PIANO · VOCAL · GUITAR

2000-2009 BEST POP SONGS

TEN YEARS OF SHEET MUSIC HITS!

Produced by
Alfred Music Publishing Co., Inc.
P.O. Box 10003
Van Nuys, CA 91410-0003
alfred.com

Printed in USA.

ISBN-10: 0-7390-6880-6
ISBN-13: 978-0-7390-6880-9

CONTENTS

1, 2, 3, 4

Words and Music by
TOM HIGGENSON

One, two, one, two, three, four.

1. Give_

1, 2, 3, 4 - 7 - 1

Verse:

21 GUNS

Lyrics by
BILLIE JOE

Music by
GREEN DAY

14 *Bridge:*

Verse 5:

5. When it's time to____ live and let die,____ and you can't____ get an -

16

21 Guns - 7 - 6

ALMOST LOVER

Words and Music by
ALISON SUDOL

Slowly (♩ = 63)

1. Your fin - ger -

(with pedal)

Verse 1:

tips a - cross my skin, the palm trees sway - ing in the wind;___ im - ag - es.___

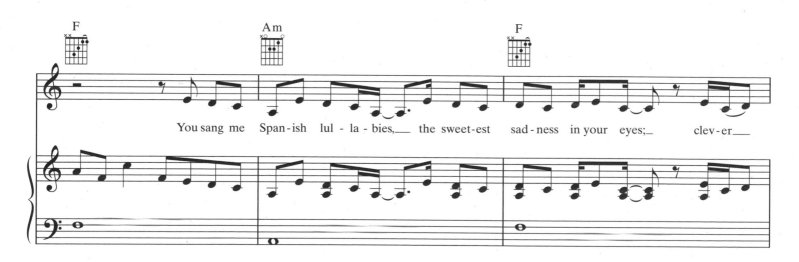

You sang me Span - ish lul - la - bies,___ the sweet - est sad - ness in your eyes;___ clev - er___

Almost Lover - 6 - 1

And when you left, you kissed my lips. You told me you would

never, never forget these im-ag-es, oh no.

Well, I'd

do.

Bridge:

I can-not go to the o-cean. I can-not drive the streets at

BE WITHOUT YOU

Words and Music by
BRYAN MICHAEL COX, JOHNTA AUSTIN,
MARY J. BLIGE, and JASON PERRY

1. Chem-is-try was cra-zy from the get - go, nei-ther one of us knew why..
2. See additional lyrics

Be Without You - 6 - 1

Bridge:

See, this is real__ talk, c -'mon, al - ways_ stay,_____ (no mat - ter what,) good or

bad,_ (thick or thin,) right or wrong (all day, ev -'ry day._____) Now if you're

down on love or don't be - lieve,_ this ain't for you.
(No,_ this ain't_ for you._____)
And if you got it

deep in your heart, and deep down you know_ that it's true,_____ well, let me see you put your
C -'mon,_ c - 'mon,_ c - 'mon._

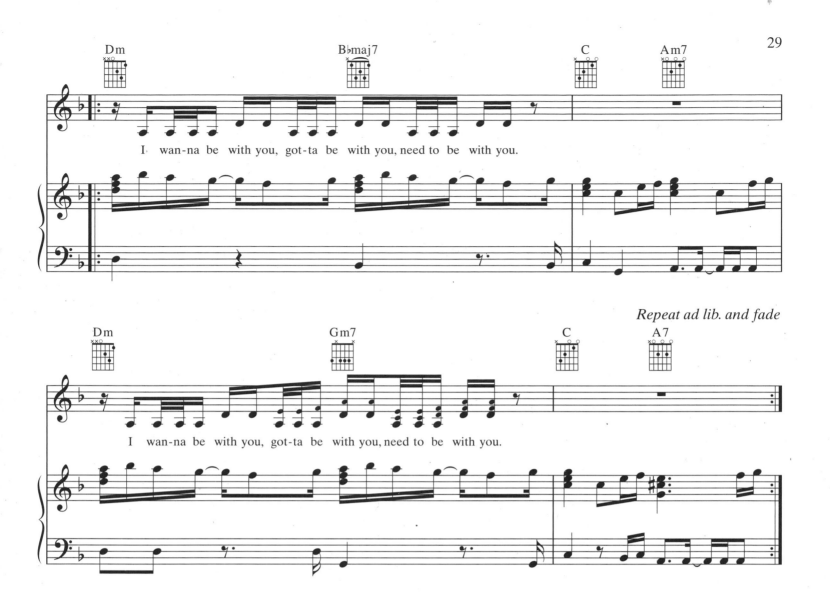

Repeat ad lib. and fade

I wan-na be with you, got-ta be with you, need to be with you.

Verse 2:
I've got a question for you,
(See, I already know the answer.)
Still, I wanna ask you:
Would you lie? *(no)*
Make me cry? *(no)*
Do somethin' behind my back and then try to cover it up?
Well, neither would I, baby.
My love is only your love, *(yes)*
I'll always be faithful. *(yes)*
I'm for real *(yes)*
And with us you'll always know the deal.
(To Chorus:)

BEAUTIFUL WORLD

(We're All Here)

Words and Music by
ADAM CROSSLEY

Moderate pop rock (♩ = 96)

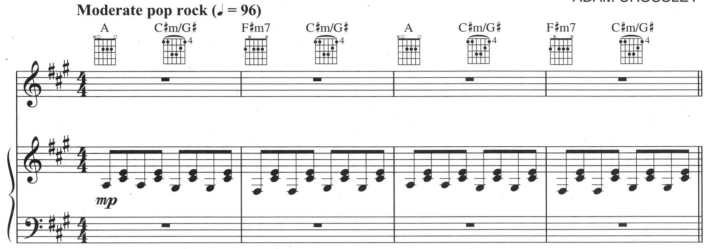

Verse 1:

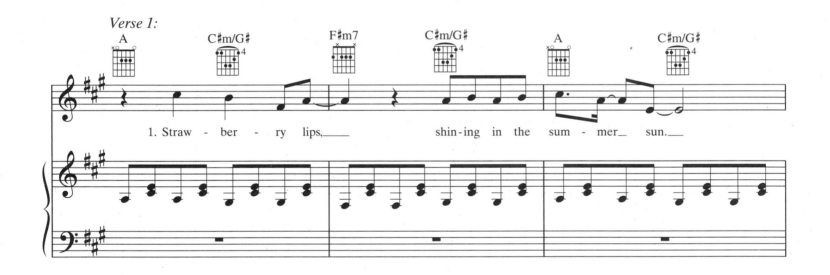

1. Straw - ber - ry lips,____ shin - ing in the sum - mer____ sun.____

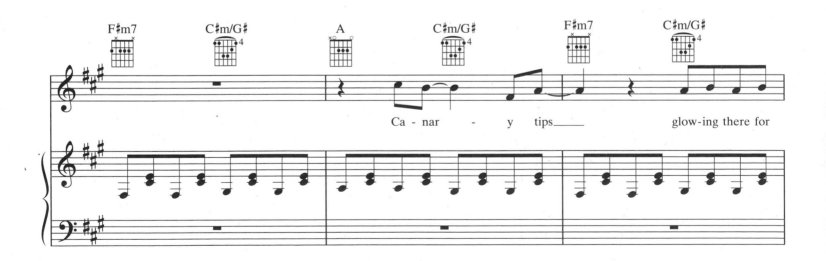

Ca - nar - y tips____ glow - ing there for

32

(Sum - mer___ sun.___) We know,___ with - in,_____ you will stay for -

ev - er___ young.___ (For - ev - er___ young.___) You fell___ a - sleep___

___ un - der___ the star - lit sea.___ It's time___ to wake up.___

% *Chorus:*

___ The moon_____ is high_____ a - bove___ you. We're all___ here 'cause___

BECAUSE OF YOU

Words and Music by
KELLY CLARKSON, BEN MOODY
and DAVID HODGES

Because of You - 6 - 1

Chorus:

you, I nev-er stray___ too far from the side - walk. Be - cause of

you, I learned to play on the safe side so I don't___ get hurt.___ Be - cause of

you, I try my hard-est just___ to for - get ev - 'ry - thing.___ Be - cause of

you, I don't know how to let___ an - y - one else___ in._____ Be - cause of you,___

BOULEVARD OF BROKEN DREAMS

Words by
BILLIE JOE

Music by
GREEN DAY

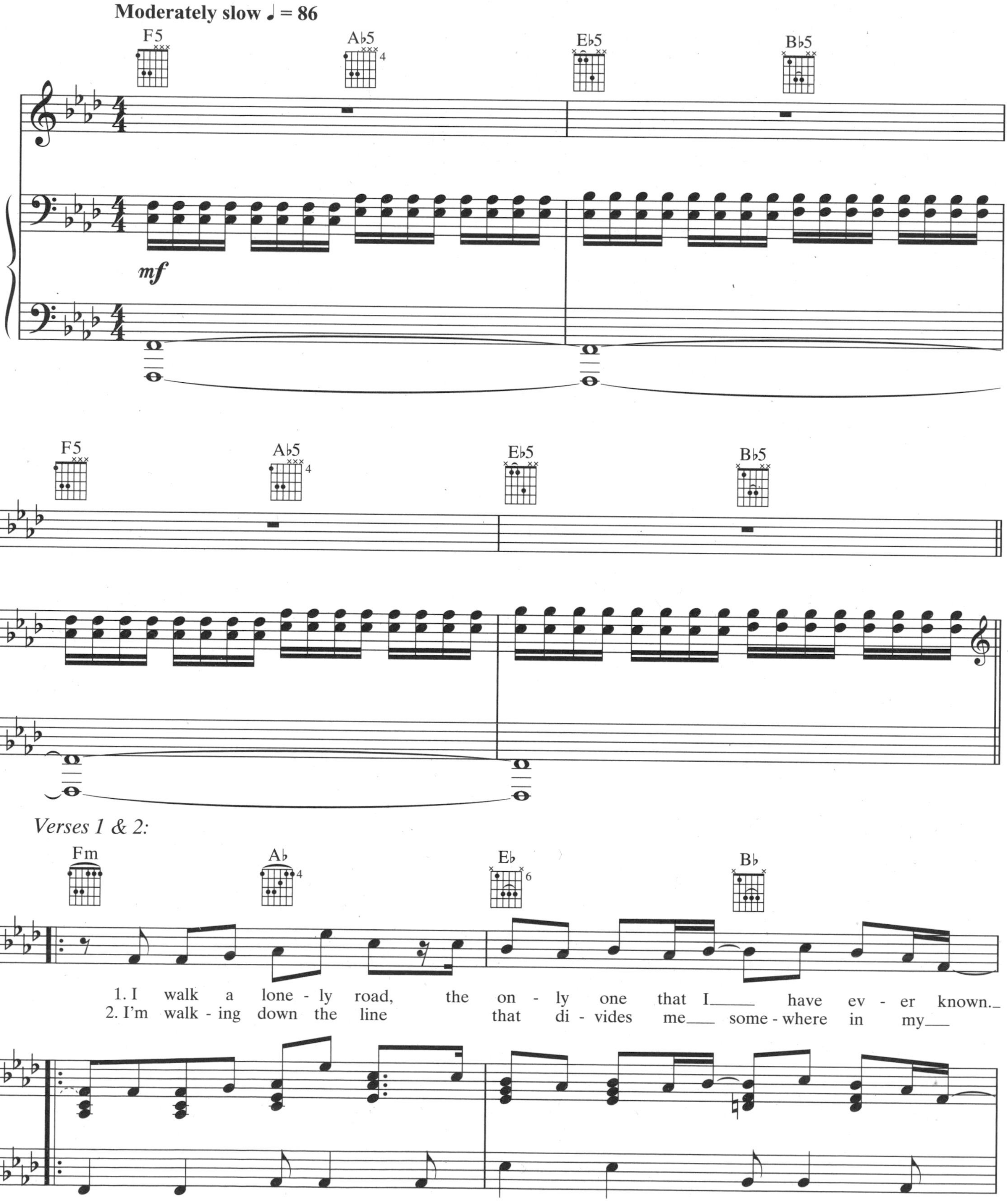
Moderately slow ♩ = 86
F5
A♭5
E♭5
B♭5
mf
F5
A♭5
E♭5
B♭5
Verses 1 & 2:
Fm
A♭
E♭
B♭
1. I walk a lone - ly road, the on - ly one that I___ have ev - er known._
2. I'm walk - ing down the line that di - vides me___ some - where in my___

44

Chorus:

To Coda

46

Boulevard of Broken Dreams - 6 - 5

where the cit - y sleeps and I'm the on - ly one___ and I walk a...

a - lone.___

CLUMSY

Words and Music by
BOBBY TROUP, WILL ADAMS
and STACY FERGUSON

Moderately ♩ = 92

(Bkgrd.) Can't help it, the girl can't help it. Oh, ba-by. Can't help it, the girl can't help it. Oh, ba-

Clumsy - 8 - 1

54

COMPLICATED

Words and Music by
LAUREN CHRISTY, GRAHAM EDWARDS,
SCOTT SPOCK and AVRIL LAVIGNE

Gtr. tuned down 1 whole step:
⑥ = D   ③ = F
⑤ = G   ② = A
④ = C   ① = D

Moderately slow rock ♩ = 80

1. Chill out, what-cha yell-ing for? Lay back, it's all been done__ be-fore.
2. You come o-ver, un-an-nounced, dressed up__ like you're some-thing else.
no. 3. (*Inst. solo ad lib....*

Complicated - 4 - 1

58

CHARIOT

Words and Music by
GAVIN DeGRAW

Verse 2:
Remember seeking moon's rebirth?
Rains made mirrors of the earth.
The sun was just yellow energy.
There is a living promise land,
Even over fields of sand.
Seasons fill my mind and cover me.
Bring it back.
More than a memory.
(To Chorus:)

CRAZY

Words and Music by
THOMAS DECARLO CALLAWAY, BRIAN JOSEPH BURTON,
GIANFRANCO REVERBERI and GIAN PIERO REVERBERI

Crazy - 5 - 1

Crazy - 5 - 3

68

Verse 2:
Come on now, who do you, who do you,
Who do you, who do you think you are?
Ha ha ha, bless your soul,
You really think you're in control.

Chorus 2:
Well, I think you're crazy.
I think you're crazy.
I think you're crazy,
Just like me.
My heroes had the heart to lose their lives out on a limb,
And all I remember is thinking I want to be like them.

Verse 3:
Ever since I was little, ever since I was little it looked like fun.
And it's no coincidence I've come,
And I can die when I'm done.

Chorus 3:
But maybe I'm crazy.
Maybe you're crazy.
Maybe we're crazy.
Probably.
(To Coda)

CRUSH

Words and Music by
EMANUEL KIRIAKOU,
DAVID HODGES and JESS CATES

Moderately slow ♩ = 84

1. I hung up the phone to-night. Some-thing hap-pened for the first time, deep in-side.

DILEMMA

Words and Music by
KENNY GAMBLE, BUNNY SIGLER,
CORNELL HAYES and ANTOINE MACON

Dilemma - 8 - 1

when I'm with__ my boo,__ boy, you know I'm cra - zy o - ver you.__ No

mat - ter what__ I do,_____ all I think a - bout__ is you.__ E - ven

when I'm with__ my boo,__ you know I'm cra - zy o - ver you.__

Verse:

(Nelly:)

1. I met this chick and she just moved right up the block from me, and
2. *See additional lyrics*

82

Verse 2:
I see a lot and you look and I never say a word.
I know how niggaz start actin' trippin' out here about they girls.
And there's no way Nelly gon' fight over no dame, as you could see.
But I like your steez, your style, your whole demeanor.
The way you come through and holla and swoop me in his two-seater.
Now that's gangstah and I got special ways to thank ya.
Don't you forget it but, it ain't that easy for you to pack up and leave him.
But you and dirty got ties for different reasons.
I respect that and right before I turn to leave, she said,
"You don't know what you mean to me."
(To Chorus:)

DANCE WITH MY FATHER

Words and Music by
RICHARD MARX and LUTHER VANDROSS

Dance With My Father - 5 - 2

88

Dance With My Father - 5 - 3

DON'T STOP THE MUSIC

Words and Music by
MICHAEL JACKSON, MIKKEL STORLEER ERIKSEN,
TOR ERIK HERMANSEN and FRANKIE STORM

Don't Stop the Music - 7 - 1

To Coda

D.S. % al Coda

se ma ma sa ma ma___ coo sa. Ma ma se ma ma sa ma ma___ coo sa,___ ma ma se ma ma sa ma ma___ coo sa.

$\oplus$ *Coda*

N.C.

Please don't stop the mu - sic.
se ma ma sa ma ma___ coo sa. Ma ma se ma ma sa ma ma___ coo sa,___ ma ma

se ma ma sa ma ma___ coo sa. Ma ma se ma ma sa ma ma___ coo sa, ma ma

Please don't stop the mu - sic.
se ma ma sa ma ma___ coo sa.

EVERYTHING

Words and Music by
MICHAEL BUBLÉ, ALAN CHANG
and AMY FOSTER

Verse:

1. You're a fall - ing star, you're the get -
ou - sel, you're a wish -

a - way car, you're the line in the sand when I go too far. You're the swim -
ing well, and you light me up when you ring my bell. You're a mys -

FALLING SLOWLY

(from *Once*)

Words and Music by
GLEN HANSARD and
MARKETA IRGLOVA

Slowly ♩ = 69

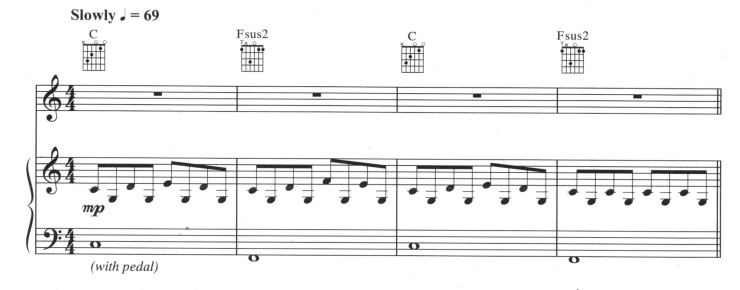

mp

(with pedal)

Verse 1:

1. I don't know you, but I want you all the more for that.

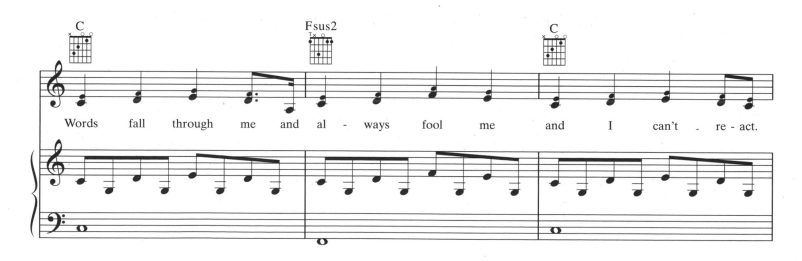

Words fall through me and al-ways fool me and I can't re-act.

Falling Slowly - 6 - 1

choice, you make it now.____

Verse 2:

2. Fall - ing slow - ly, eyes that know me and I can't go back.

Moods that take me and e - rase me and I'm paint - ed black.

Well, you have suf-fered e - nough and warred with your -

FAMILY AFFAIR

Words and Music by
ANDRE YOUNG, MELVIN BRADFORD,
MARY J. BLIGE, MICHAEL ELIZONDO,
CAMARA KAMBON, LUCHANA LODGE,
ASIAH LOUIS and BRUCE MILLER

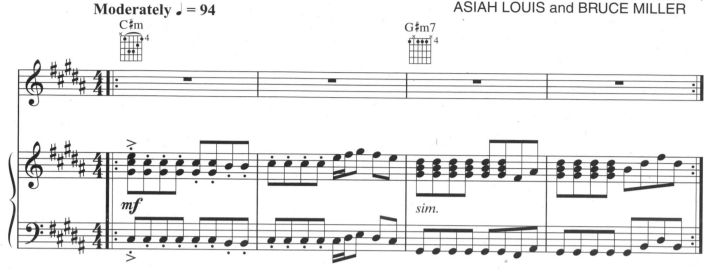

Let's get it crunk up - on, have fun up - on, up in this danc - er -

y. We got y'all o - pen now, ya float - in' so ya gots to dance for

Family Affair - 7 - 1

Verse 3:

Chorus:

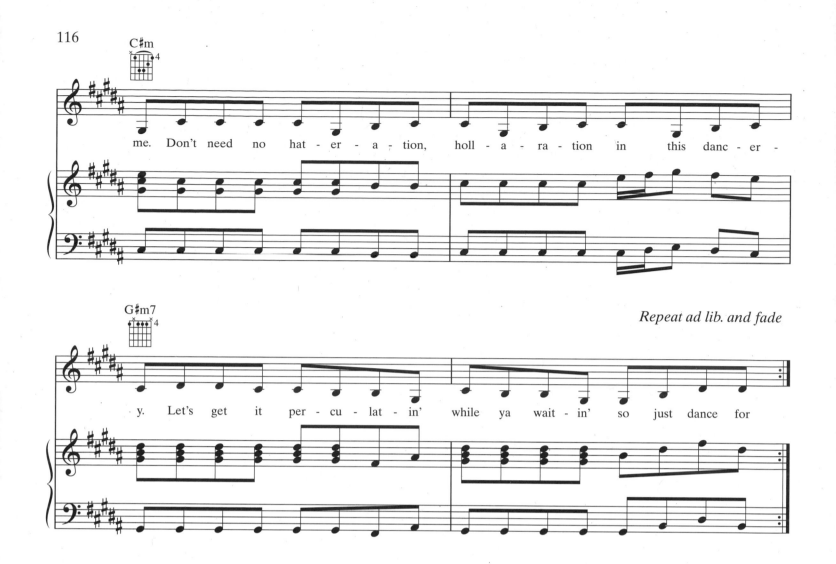

Verse 2:
It's only going to be about a matter of time
Before ya get loose and start to lose your mind.
Cop you a drink, go ahead and rock ya ice,
'Cause we're celebrating no more drama in our life.
With the Dre track pumpin', everybody's jumpin'.
Go ahead and twist ya back and get body bumpin'.
I told ya, leave your situations at the door.
So grab somebody and get your ass on the dance floor.
(To Chorus:)

THE GAME OF LOVE

(featuring Michelle Branch)

Words and Music by
GREGG ALEXANDER and RICK NOWELS

118

So, please tell me (1.3.) why___ don't you come a-round___
So, please, ba - by, (2.) try___ and use me for what___

___ no more.___ 'Cause right now I'm { 1. cry 3. dy } -
___ I'm good___ for.___ It ain't say - ing good - bye,___

ing ing } ___ out - side the door of your { 1. can - dy 3. lov - ing } store. } It just takes a
it's knock-ing down the door of your can - dy store. }

Chorus:

lit - tle bit of this, a lit - tle bit of that. It start - ed with a kiss, now we're___

The Game of Love - 5 - 2

in the game_ of love._____ It's all_____ in this game_ of love._

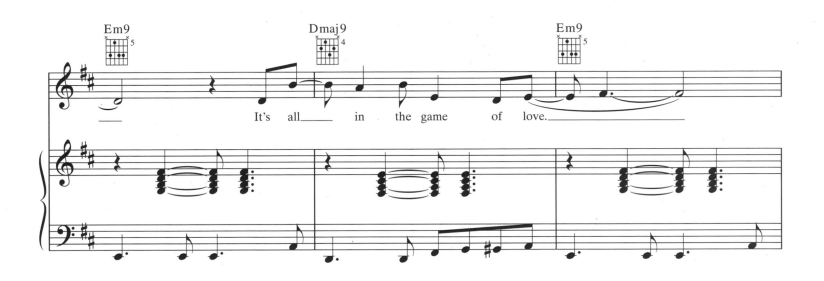

_____ It's all_____ in the game of love._____

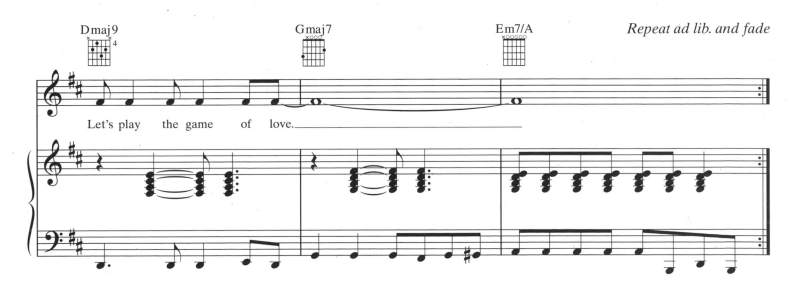

Repeat ad lib. and fade

Let's play the game of love._____

GOLD DIGGER

Words and Music by
RAY CHARLES, RENALD RICHARD
and KANYE WEST

Moderately ♩ = 108

N.C.

She take my mon - ey when I'm in need.___ Yeah, she's a

tri - flin' friend in - deed.__ Oh, she's a gold dig - ger way o - ver

Rap beat ♩ = 92

𝄋 *Chorus:*
A♭7

town__ that digs on me. She gives me mon - ey when I'm in need.
(Rap:) Now, I ain't say-in' she's a gold dig-ger,

Gold Digger - 5 - 1

⊕ *Coda*

leave._____ Yeah,_ she gives me mon - ey.

Verse 2:
Eighteen years, eighteen years,
She got one of your kids, got you for eighteen years.
I know somebody payin' child support for one of his kids.
His baby momma's car and crib is bigger than his.
You will see him on TV any given Sunday.
Win the Super Bowl and drive off in a Hyundai.
She was s'pposed to buy your shorty Tyco with your money.
She went to the doctor, got lypo with your money.
She walkin' around, lookin' like Michael with your money.
Should of got that insured, Geico for your money.
If you ain't no punk, holler, "We want prenup."
We want prenup, yeah.
It's something that you need to have,
'Cause when she leave your ass she gone leave with half.
Eighteen years, eighteen years,
And on her 18th birthday, he found out it wasn't his.
(To Chorus:)

Verse 3:
Now, I ain't sayin' you a gold digger, you got needs.
You don't want your dude to smoke, but he can't buy weed.
You go out to eat and he can't pay, ya'll can't leave.
There's dishes in the back, he gotta roll up his sleeves.
But why ya'll washin', watch him.
He gone make it into a Benz out of that Datsun.
He got that ambition, baby, look in his eyes.
This week he moppin' floors, next week it's the fries.
So, stick by his side.
I know his dude's ballin' but, yeah, that's nice.
And they gone keep callin' and tryin',
But you stay right, girl.
But when you get on, he leave your ass for a white girl.
(To Chorus:)

GRADUATION
(Friends Forever)

Words and Music by
COLLEEN FITZPATRICK
and JOSH DEUTSCH

1. So we talked all night a-bout the rest of our lives, where we're gon-na be when we turn twen-ty - five. I keep think-ing times will nev-er change,_ keep on think-ing things will nev-er be the same. But when we

Graduation - 7 - 1

me and you__ and when we got real blue,__ we'd stay at home,__ talk-ing on__ the tel - e-phone, and we would

get so ex - cit - ed and we'd get so scared,__ laugh-ing at our-selves, think-ing life's not fair.

Chorus:

And this is how it feels... As we go on, we re - mem - ber

all the times we had to - geth - er. And as our lives change,

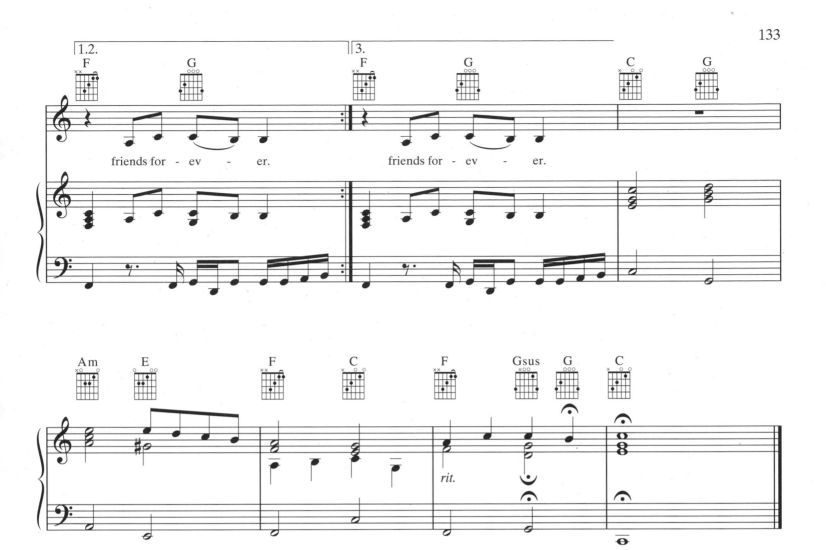

Verse 2:
So if we get the big jobs and we make the big money,
When we look back at now, will our jokes still be funny?
Will we still remember everything we learned in school,
Still be trying to break every single rule?
Will little brainy Bobby be the stockbroker man?
Can Heather find a job that won't interfere with her tan?
I keep, keep thinking that it's not goodbye,
Keep on thinking it's our time to fly.
And this is how it feels…
(To Chorus:)

Verse 3:
Will we think about tomorrow like we think about now?
Can we survive it out there, can we make it somehow?
I guess I thought that this would never end,
And suddenly it's like we're women and men.
Will the past be a shadow that will follow us around?
Will the memories fade when I leave this town?
I keep, keep thinking that it's not goodbye,
Keep thinking it's our time to fly.
(To Chorus:)

HAVEN'T MET YOU YET

Words and Music by
MICHAEL BUBLÉ, ALAN CHANG
and AMY FOSTER

Haven't Met You Yet - 8 - 1

Haven't Met You Yet - 8 - 5

HIPS DON'T LIE

Lyrics by
SHAKIRA and WYCLEF JEAN

Music by
WYCLEF JEAN, JERRY DUPLESSIS, SHAKIRA,
OMAR ALFANNO and LATAVIA PARKER

Moderate latin feel (♩ = 100)

Hips Don't Lie - 10 - 1

◍ *Coda*

Chorus:

Verse 2:

2. Oh, boy, I can see your bod - y mov - ing;___ half an - i - mal, half___ man.___

I don't, don't real - ly know what I'm do - ing___ but you seem to have a___ plan.___

My___ will and self - re - straint___ have___ come to fail___ now, fail___ now.

See, I'm do - ing what I can, but I can't_ so you know. That's a bit too hard to ex - plain._

Vocal Break:

Oh, ba - by, when you talk like that, you know you got me hyp - no - tized._

So be__ wise and keep__ on read - ing the signs of my bod - y.

Bridge:

Se - ño - ri - ta, feel the con - ga, let me see you move like you come from Co - lom - bia.

Mi - ra en Ba - rran-qui - lla   se bai - la a - sí, say   it! Mi - ra en Ba - rran-qui - lla   se bai-la a - sí.

Rap:

Yeah, she's so sexy, every man's fantasy, a refugee like me back with the Fugees from a third world country.

I go back like when 'pac carried crates for Humpty Humpty. I need a whole club dizzy.

Why the C.I.A. wanna watch us? Colombians and Haitians, I ain't guilty, it's a musical transaction.

Ho-bope, se-bope, no more do we snatch ropes. Refugees run the seas 'cause we own our own boats.

Chorus:

I'm on to-night,__ my hips don't lie and I'm start-ing to feel__ you, boy.

Come on, let's go_____ real slow. Ba - by, like this is per - fec - to.

HOT N' COLD

Words and Music by
KATY PERRY, LUKASZ GOTTWALD
and MAX MARTIN

Hot n' Cold - 6 - 1

HEY THERE DELILAH

Words and Music by
TOM HIGGENSON

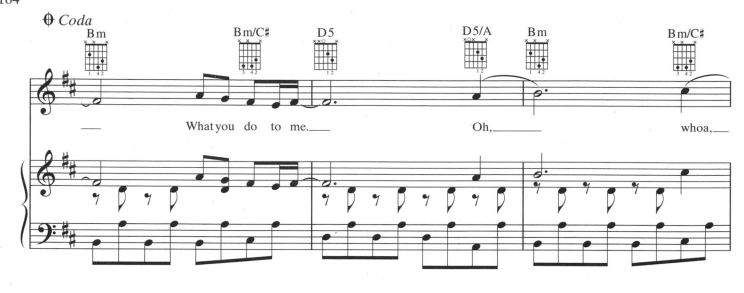

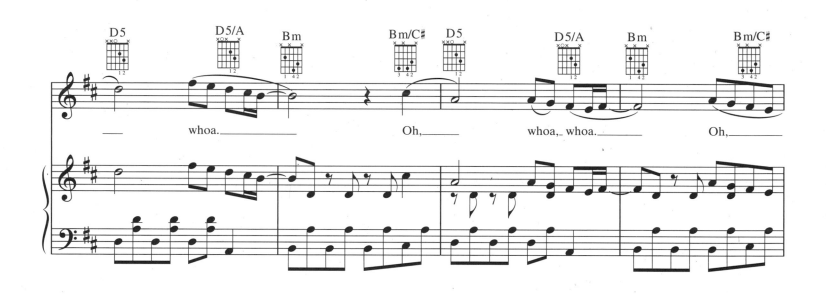

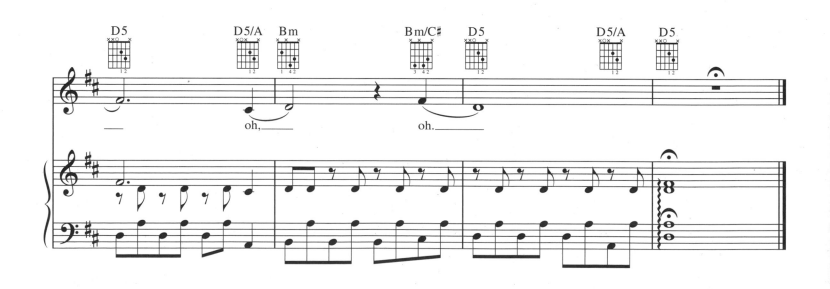

I DIDN'T KNOW MY OWN STRENGTH

Words and Music by
DIANE WARREN

1. Lost touch with my soul. I had no-where to turn, I had no-where to go.
2. Found hope in my heart. I found the light to light my way out of the dark.

Lost sight of my dream. Thought it would be the end of me.
Found all that I need here in-side of me.

I thought I'd nev-er make it through. I had no hope to hold on to. I,
I thought I'd nev-er find my way. I thought I'd nev-er lift that weight. I,

I KISSED A GIRL

Words and Music by
KATY PERRY, LUKASZ GOTTWALD,
MAX MARTIN and CATHY DENNIS

I Kissed a Girl - 4 - 1

I TURN TO YOU

Words and Music by
DIANE WARREN

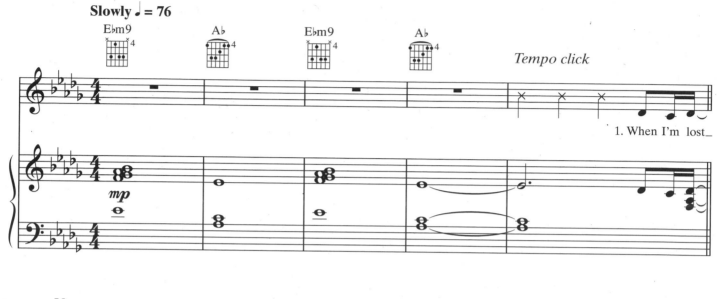

I Turn to You - 6 - 1

Chorus:

IF EVERYONE CARED

Lyrics by
CHAD KROEGER

Music by
NICKELBACK

If Everyone Cared - 5 - 1

If Everyone Cared - 5 - 2

D.S. % al Coda

INSIDE YOUR HEAVEN

Words and Music by
ANDREAS CARLSSON, PER NYLEN
and SAVAN KOTECHA

Inside Your Heaven - 5 - 1

Chorus:

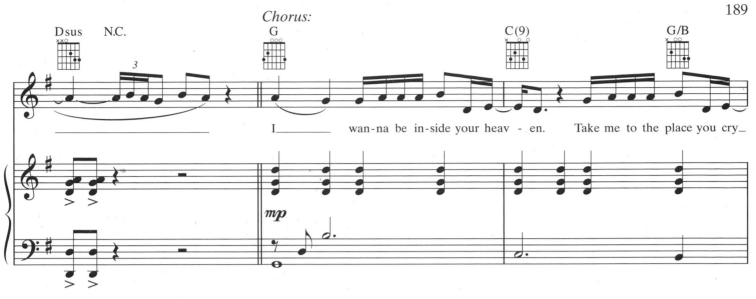

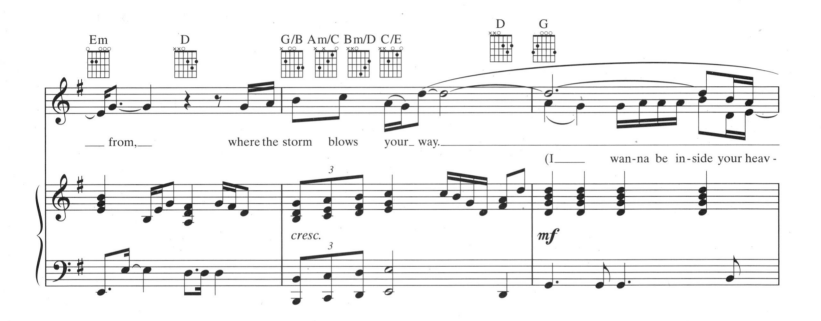

LEAVIN'

Words and Music by
TERIUS NASH, CORRON COLE, JAMES BUNTON
and CHRISTOPHER STEWART

Moderate groove ♩ = 80

1. Hey, ba-by girl,__ I been watch-in' you all__ day, all__ day, all__ day, all__ day.
2. Now, if I talk it, girl, you know that I will walk it out, walk it out, walk it out, walk it out.

Man, that thing you got be-hind you is a - maz - in', a - maz - in', a - maz - in', a - maz - in'.
Man, I'll put my mon-ey, mon - ey where my mouth__ is,__ mouth__ is,__ mouth__ is,__ mouth__ is.

LIVE YOUR LIFE

Words and Music by
CLIFFORD HARRIS, MAKEBA RIDDICK,
JUSTIN SMITH and MIHAI BALAN DAN

Moderately slow ♩ = 84

Mi - ya hee,_____ mi - ya ho,_____ mi - ya hu,_____

mi - ya ha - ha. Mi - ya hee,_____ mi - ya ho,_____ mi - ya hu,_____

Ay, it's special what's happenin' to all my,

mi - ya ha - ha. Mi - ya hee,_____ mi - ya ho,_____ mi - ya hu,_____

all my soldiers over there in Iraq.   *Everybody right here,*   *what you need to do...*

Instead of being gracious, they violate in a major way.   *I never been a hater, still I love them in a crazy way.*

G **D**

Some say they sold the yay and know they couldn't get work on Labor Day. *It ain't that black and white, it has an area the shade of gray.*

A **Bm** **G** **D**

I'm Westside anyway, even if I left today and stayed away.   *Some move away to make a way, not move away 'cause they afraid.*

A **Bm** **G** **D**

I brought back to the hood and all you ever did was take away. *I pray for patience, but they make me wanna melt their face away.*

mi - ya ha__ ha. Mi - ya hee,__ __ mi - ya ha__ ha. So live your life.__

Verse 2:
I'm the opposite of moderate, immaculately polished with
The spirit of a hustler and the swagger of a college kid.
Allergic to the counterfeit, impartial to the politics,
*Articulate, but still I'll grab a n***** by the collar quick.*

Whoever having problems with their record sales just holla till.
If that don't work and all else fails, then turn around and follow till.
I got love for the game but, ay, I'm not in love with all of it.
'Could do without the fame and the rappers nowadays are comedy.

The hootin' and the hollerin', back and forth with the arguing,
Where you from, who you know, what you make, and what kind of car you in.
Seems as though you lost sight of what's important when depositin'
Them checks into your bank account and you up out of poverty.

Your values is a disarray, prioritizing horribly,
Unhappy with your riches 'cause you're piss-poor morally,
Ignoring all prior advice and forewarning.
And we mighty full of ourselves all of a sudden, aren't we?
(To Chorus:)

MY IMMORTAL

Words and Music by
BEN MOODY, AMY LEE
and DAVID HODGES

Slowly and freely ♩ = 80

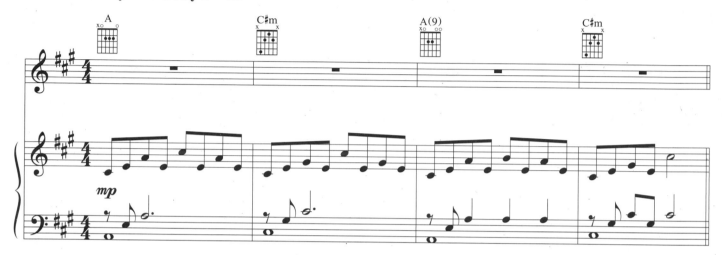

Verse:

1. I'm so tired of be - ing here,___
2. *See additional lyrics*

sup - pressed___ by all___ my

child - ish fears.___

And if you have to leave,___

My Immortal - 5 - 1

C♯m
A(9)
I wish that you would just leave, 'cause your presence still lingers here,
C♯m
F♯m
C♯m 4fr.
and it won't leave me alone. These wounds won't seem to heal.
F♯m
C♯m 4fr.
F♯m
C♯m 4fr.
E
Esus
E
This pain is just too real. There's just too much that time cannot erase.
Chorus:
F♯m
E/D
Esus/D
E
C♯m 4fr.
When you cried, I'd wipe away all of your tears.

Verse 2:
You used to captivate me
By your resonating light.
But, now I'm bound by the life you left behind.
Your face, it haunts
My once pleasant dreams.
Your voice, it chased away
All the sanity in me.
These wounds won't seem to heal.
This pain is just too real.
There's just too much that time can not erase.
(To Chorus:)

MY LIFE WOULD SUCK WITHOUT YOU

Words and Music by
CLAUDE KELLY, LUKASZ GOTTWALD
and MAX MARTIN

1. Guess this means you're sor -
2. Ba - by, I was stu -

My Life Would Suck Without You - 7 - 1

NEW SOUL

Words and Music by
YAEL NAIM and DAVID DONATIEN

Verses 1 & 2:

1. I'm a new soul, I came to this strange world, hop-ing I could
   young soul in this ver-y strange world, hop-ing I could

learn a bit 'bout how to give and take._ But since I came here, felt the joy and
learn a bit 'bout what is true and fake._ But why all this_ hate? Try to com-mu-

the fear, find-ing my-self mak-ing ev'ry pos-si-ble mis-take._
ni-cate, find-ing trust and love is not al-ways eas-y to make._

La la

Chorus:

la   la,   la la la la   la___ la,   la la la la   la,___ la la la,___ la la

la.___   La la la la,   la la la la   la___ la,   la la la la

la,___ la la la,___ la la   la.___   2. See I'm a   la.___   Ooh.___

Bridge:

This is a hap - py end,_____

'cause you don't un - - der-stand

ev - 'ry-thing you___ have done._____

Now why's ev - 'ry - thing___ so wrong?_

Verse 3:

This is a hap - py end.___ Come and give me your hand.

I'll take you far___ a - way.___ 3. I'm a new soul, I came to this

strange world hop - ing I could learn a bit 'bout how to give and take.___ But since I

came here, felt the joy and the fear, find - ing my - self mak - ing ev - 'ry pos - si - ble mis -

ONE STEP AT A TIME

Words and Music by
MICH HANSEN, JONAS JEBERG,
ROBBIE NEVIL and LAUREN EVANS

*Original recording in D♭ major.

One Step At a Time - 6 - 1

Chorus:

step at a time.__ There's no need to rush.__ It's like learn-ing to fly__ or

fall-ing in love.__ It's gon-na hap-pen and it's sup-posed to hap-pen that we

find the rea-sons why,__ one step at a time.__ Da da da da da da

da da da da n da da. Da da da da da da da da da da n da da.

PARTY IN THE U.S.A.

Words and Music by
CLAUDE KELLY, LUKASZ GOTTWALD
and JESSICA CORNISH

Moderately ♩ = 96

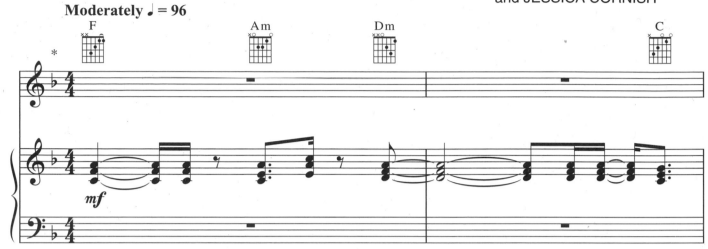

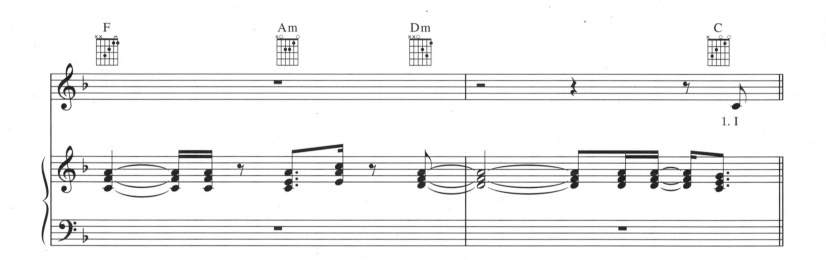

Verse:

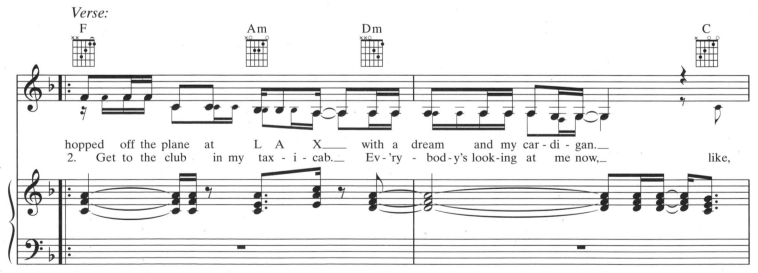

hopped off the plane at L A X___ with a dream and my car - di - gan.___
2. Get to the club in my tax - i - cab.___ Ev - ’ry - bod - y’s look - ing at me now,___ like,

*Recording in F♯ major.

Party in the U.S.A. - 6 - 1

Gtr. tuned down 1/2 step:
⑥ = E♭ ③ = G♭
⑤ = A♭ ② = B♭
④ = D♭ ① = E♭

PHOTOGRAPH

Lyrics by
CHAD KROEGER

Music by
NICKELBACK

good - bye,___ good - bye._____ Look at this pho - to - graph._

___ Ev-'ry time I do, it makes me laugh.___ Ev-'ry time I do, it makes me…

SMILE

Words and Music by
MATTHEW SHAFER, BLAIR DALY,
J.T. HARDING and JEREMY BOSE

Smile - 6 - 1

SOAK UP THE SUN

Words and Music by
SHERYL CROW and JEFF TROTT

Moderately fast ♩ = 120

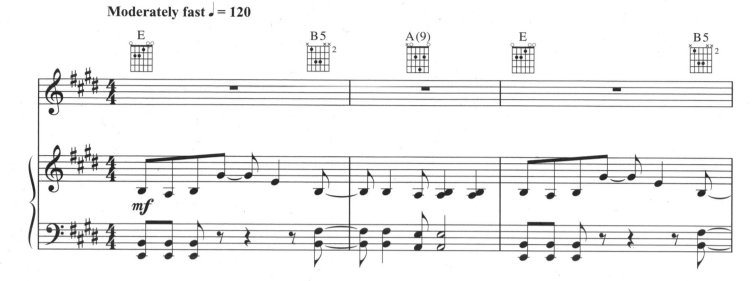

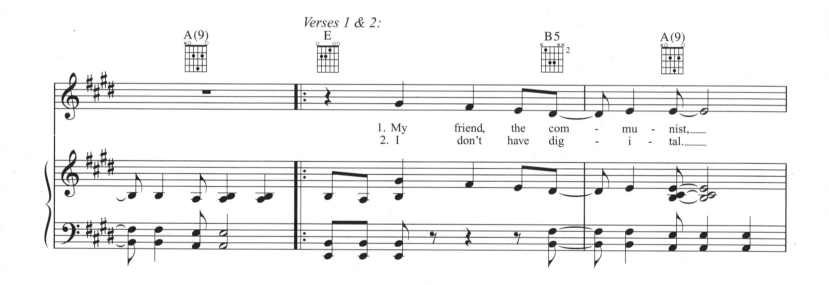

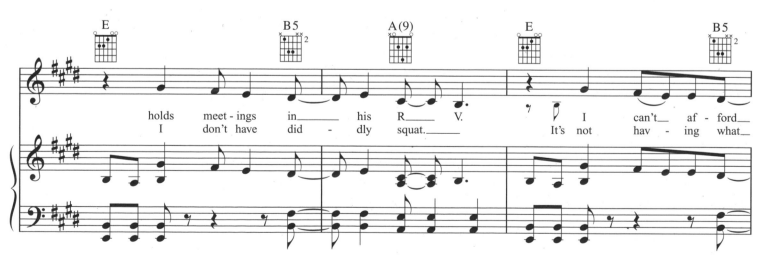

B
E
up.
(I'm gon - na tell 'em that)
I've
B
got no one to blame.
For ev - 'ry time I feel
F♯m
A
B
lame I'm look - ing up.
E
B5
A(9)
I'm gon - na soak up the sun
I'm gon - na soak up the

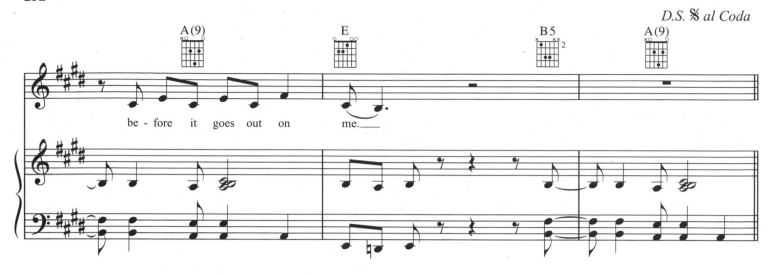

be - fore it goes out on me.

Coda

I'm_____ gon - na soak up the sun,_____

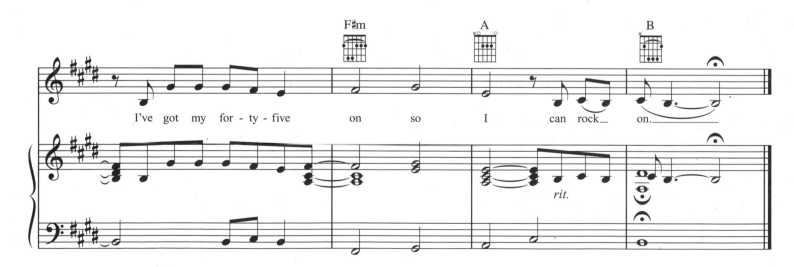

I've got my for - ty - five on so I can rock_ on._____

rit.

STICKWITU

Words and Music by
FRANNE GOLDE, ROBERT PALMER
and KASIA LIVINGSTON

Slowly ♩ = 72

Verses 1 & 2:

1. I don't wan-na go___ an-oth-er day,___ so I'm
2. *See additional lyrics*

tell-ing you ex-act-ly what is on my mind. Seems like

Stickwitu - 7 - 1

Chorus:

Bridge:

Verse 3:

3. So, don't you wor-ry a - bout_ peo-ple hang-in' a - round._ They ain't bring-in' us down._ I
yeah.)

know you and you know me and that's all that_ counts.

So don't be wor-ried a - bout_ peo-ple hang-in' a - round._ They ain't bring-in' us down._ I

know you and you know me and that's, that's why_ I say... Hey,_

Chorus:

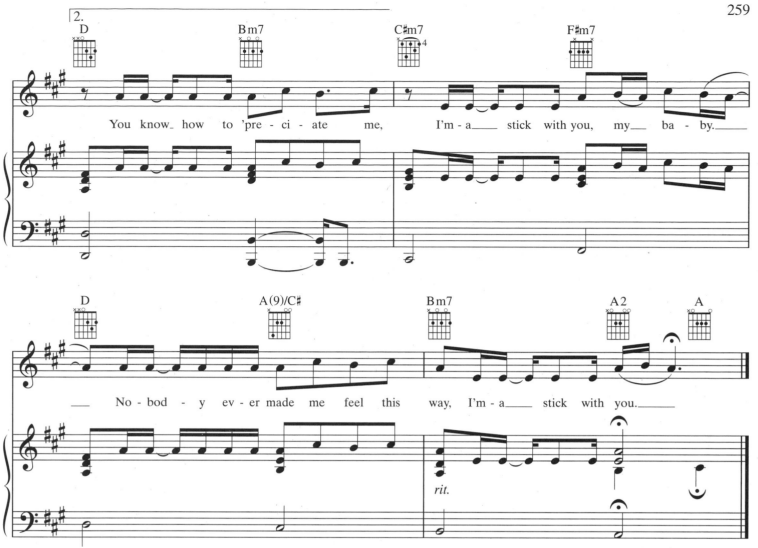

Verse 2:
I don't want to go another day,
So, I'm telling you exactly what is on my mind.
See, the way we ride in our private lives,
Ain't nobody getting in between.
I want you to know that you're the only one for me.
And I say…
(To Chorus:)

THE STORY

Words and Music by
PHIL HANSEROTH

Moderately ♩ = 96

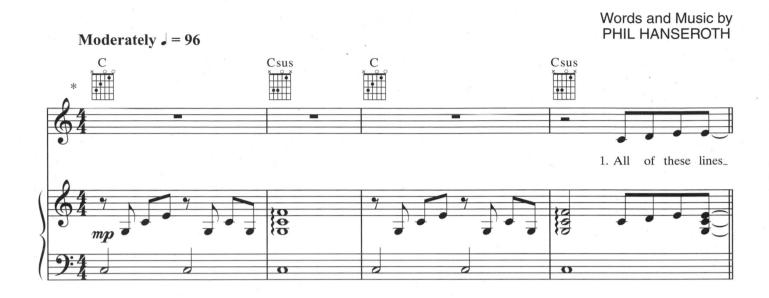

1. All of these lines_

Verse 1:

_ a-cross_ my face_ tell you the sto - ry of who I am._

_ So man-y_ sto - ries of where I've been_ and how I got_

*Original recording in B major, with guitar tuned down a half step.

Verse 4:

4. You see the smile____ that's on____ my mouth?____ It's hid-ing the words___
...end solo)

____ that don't____ come____ out.____ All of my___ friends___ who think__ that I'm blessed,___

____ they don't___ know___ my head___ is a mess.____ No,

they don't know_ who I_____ real-ly am.____ And they don't know_ what I've_

THIS IS IT

Written and Composed by
MICHAEL JACKSON
and PAUL ANKA

UMBRELLA

Words and Music by
**TERIUS NASH, SHAWN CARTER,
THADDIS HARRELL** and
CHRISTOPHER STEWART

Moderately ♩ = 92

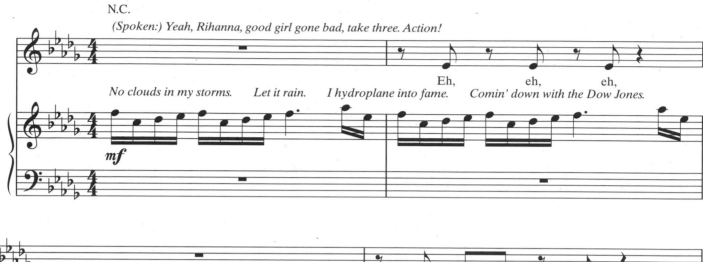

Umbrella - 7 - 1

Chorus:

WE BELONG TOGETHER

Words and Music by
KENNETH EDMONDS, DARNELL BRISTOL, SIDNEY JOHNSON,
JOHNTA AUSTIN, JERMAINE DUPRI, MANUEL SEAL, SANDRA SULLY,
MARIAH CAREY, PATRICK MOTEN and BOBBY WOMACK

We Belong Together - 7 - 1

Verse 1:

1. I did-n't mean it when I said I did-n't love you so. I should have held on tight, I nev-er should have let you go.

I did-n't know noth-ing, I was stu-pid, I was fool-ish, I was ly-in' to my-self.___

I could-n't have fath-omed I would ev-er be with-out your love. Nev-er i-mag-ined I'd be sit-ting here be-side my-self.

Guess I did-n't know you, 'cause I did-n't know me, but I thought I knew ev-'ry-thing. I nev-er felt___

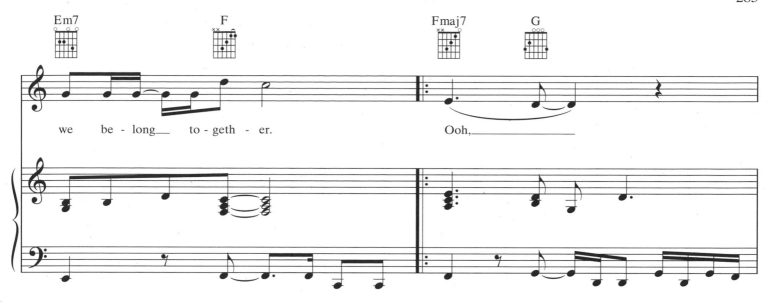

we be-long__ to-geth-er.   Ooh,_____

Repeat ad lib. and fade

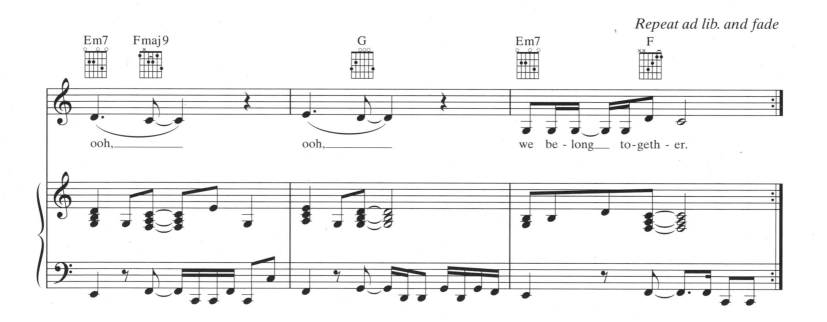

ooh,_____   ooh,_____   we be-long__ to-geth-er.

WHAT ABOUT NOW

Words and Music by
BEN MOODY, DAVID HODGES
and JOSH HARTZLER

Verses 2 & 3:

𝄋 *Chorus:*

WHAT GOES AROUND... COMES AROUND

Words and Music by
TIM MOSLEY, NATE HILLS
and JUSTIN TIMBERLAKE

Slowly ♩ = 72

What Goes Around... Comes Around - 7 - 1

WHATEVER YOU LIKE

Words and Music by
CLIFFORD HARRIS, DAVID SIEGEL
and JAMES SCHEFFER

Whatever You Like - 7 - 1

Whatever You Like - 7 - 2

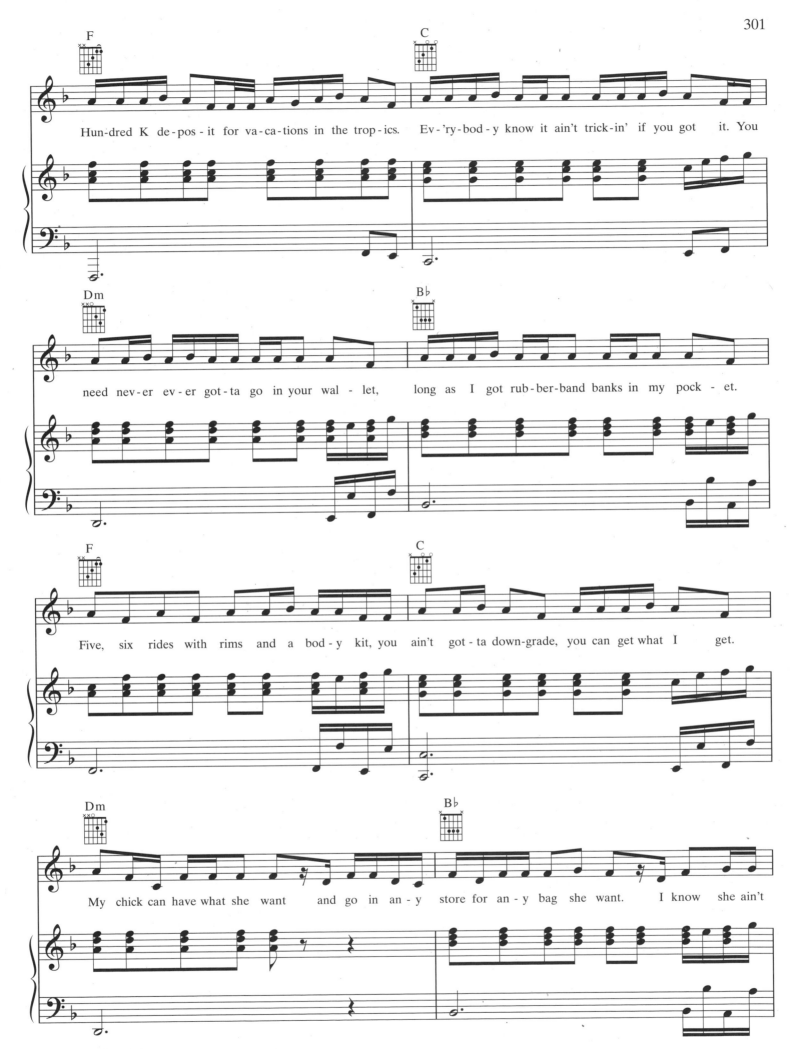

nev - er had a man like that, to buy you an - y - thing your heart de - sires like that. Yeah, I

want your bod - y, need your bod - y. Long as you got me, you won't need no - bod - y. You

D.S. ℅ al Coda

want it, I got it, go get it, I'll buy it. Tell them oth - er broke n**-**** be qui - et. Stacks on

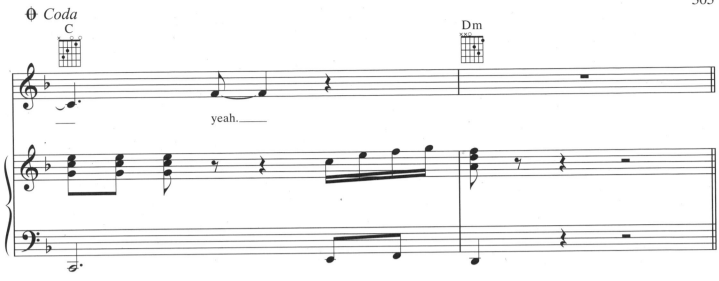

Repeat ad lib. and fade

WILD HORSES

Words and Music by
MICK JAGGER and KEITH RICHARDS

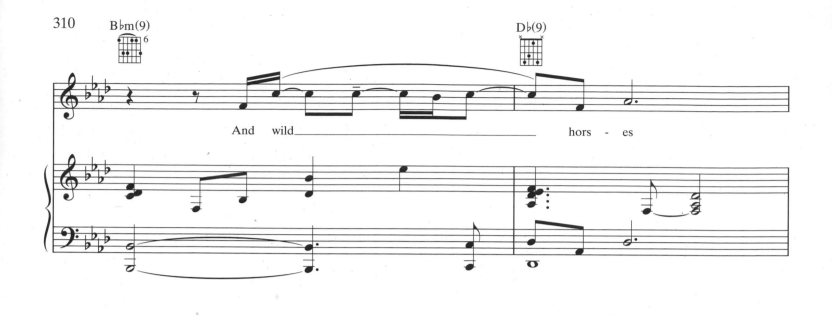

And wild_____ hors - es

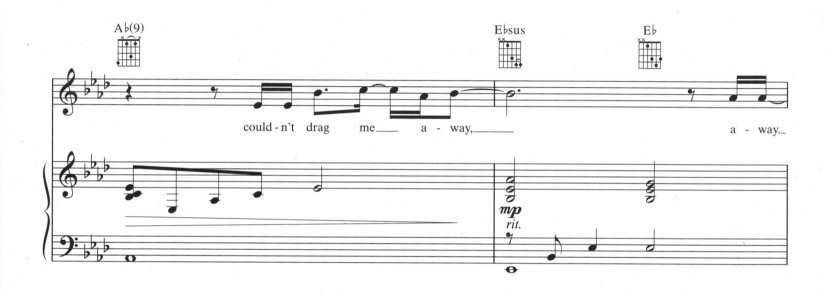

could - n't drag me___ a - way,_____ a - way._

Freely

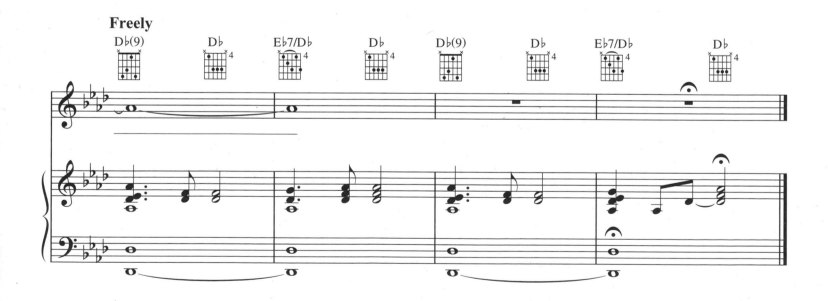

YOU RAISE ME UP

Words and Music by
ROLF LOVLAND and
BRENDAN GRAHAM

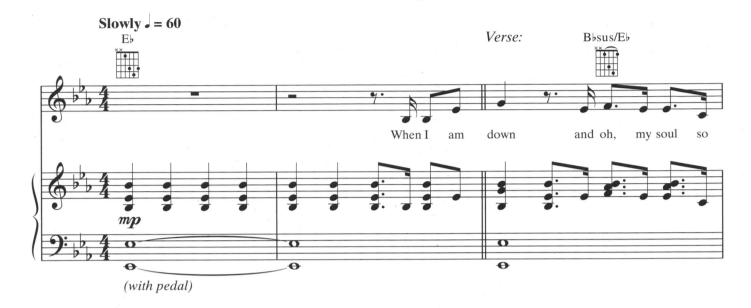

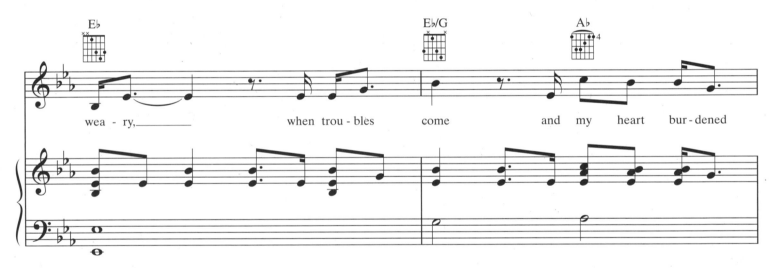

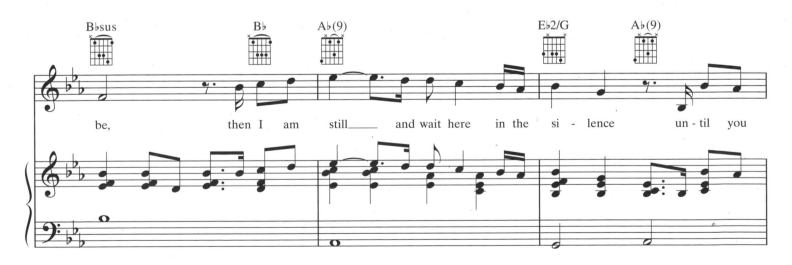

You Raise Me Up - 5 - 1

Chorus:

YOU PULLED ME THROUGH

Words and Music by
DIANE WARREN

318

You Pulled Me Through - 4 - 3

BRINGING YOU OVER 48,000 TITLES OF TODAY'S HITS AND YESTERDAY'S CLASSICS!

Working on a Dream
Bruce Springsteen
(00-32204)
Book, $19.95

Greatest Hits
Bruce Springsteen
(00-PF9541)
Book, $19.95

Mothership
Led Zeppelin
(00-30381)
Book, $24.95

Dream Theater Keyboard Experience
Dream Theater featuring Jordan Rudess
(00-32032)
Book, $26.95

The Van Halen Keyboard Songbook
Van Halen
(00-27506)
Book, $14.95

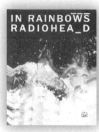

In Rainbows
Radiohead
(00-29220)
Book, $19.95

One of the Boys
Katy Perry
(00-31810)
Book, $16.95

Wincing the Night Away
The Shins
(00-28009)
Book, $19.95

American Idiot
Green Day
(00-PFM0506)
Book, $19.95

The Open Door
Evanescence
(00-27640)
Book, $19.95

Vampire Weekend
Vampire Weekend
(00-30733)
Book, $19.95

The Lost Christmas Eve
Trans-Siberian Orchestra
(00-30552) Book, $21.95

SELECTIONS FROM TODAY'S BOX OFFICE HITS

Harry Potter Musical Magic: The First Five Years
Music from Motion Pictures 1-5
(00-32033)
Book, $19.95

The Lord of the Rings: The Fellowship of the Ring
Music by Howard Shore
(00-0659B)
Book, $14.95

Corpse Bride: Selections from the Motion Picture
Music by Danny Elfman
(00-27925)
Book, $16.95

Star Wars: A Musical Journey (Music from Episodes I – VI)
Music by John Williams
(00-28303)
Book, $19.95

The Dark Knight: Selections from the Motion Picture
(00-31866)
Book, $14.95

Indiana Jones and the Kingdom of the Crystal Skull: Selections from the Motion Picture
Music by John Williams
(00-31379)
Book, $12.95

AVAILABLE at YOUR FAVORITE MUSIC RETAILER